Down with heaven

Down with heaven

Ian Barclay

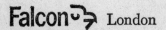 London

First published 1975
Copyright © Ian Barclay 1975

ISBN 0 85491 550 8

Quotations from the Bible, unless otherwise stated,
are from the Revised Standard Version, copyrighted
in 1952 and 1946.

FALCON BOOKS
are published by the Church Pastoral Aid Society,
Falcon Court, 32 Fleet Street, London EC4Y 1DB.

Overseas agents
EMU Book Agencies Ltd, 63 Berry Street,
Granville 2142, NSW, Australia.

Sunday School Centre Wholesale,
PO Box 3020, Cape Town, South Africa.

Scripture Union Bookshop, PO Box 760,
Wellington, New Zealand.

Anglican Book Society, 228 Bank Street,
Ottawa K2P 1X1, Canada.

Made and printed in Great Britain by
Hunt Barnard Printing Ltd, Aylesbury, Bucks.

Contents

The fruit of the Spirit

As a family we recently visited an attractive Elizabethan manor house in Hampshire, called Braemore House. As you leave the front door you are immediately confronted with a wall almost hidden by a luxuriant growth that has been trained along it over the years. It is so magnificent that, not surprisingly, the children wanted to know what sort of tree it was. Even on a wet August afternoon, the answer was simple because the green figs were so conspicuous. We were holidaying in the New Forest, and time and again unknown trees were identified by their fruit. Even in the garden of our holiday cottage trees identified themselves by the fruit hanging from their branches. It is an invariable rule that apples grow on apple trees while figs grow on fig trees. Nature knows no exception to this principle.

Jesus said, 'Are grapes gathered from thorns, or figs from thistles? So, every sound tree bears good fruit, but the bad tree bears evil fruit. A sound tree cannot bear evil fruit, nor can a bad tree bear good fruit' (Matthew 7.16,17).

The *Fruit of the Spirit* is the way by which the Christian life can be identified. The testimony that a man gives, the denomination to which he belongs, the positions that he holds in a particular church say nothing about his spiritual life. The only real evidence that we have is the fruit that the Spirit plants and causes to grow. As pears identify pear trees, so love, joy, peace, patience, kindness, goodness, faithfulness, gentleness and self-control (Galatians 5.22) identify the Christian life; it is as simple as that.

To expect to see the fruit of the Spirit in the life of each believer may appear to be expecting the impossible, but this is clearly what the New Testament expects. The display of this fruit is not the result of more faith, a second blessing, a closer walk, a higher life, or a more frantic fanaticism. It is simply the result of *normal Christian living*. And it is undoubtedly the normal Christian life that the world desperately needs to see today. A good deal of the scepticism that the world has about Christianity is largely due to the fact that it has never seen real Christianity in action. Love, joy, peace, patience, kindness, goodness, faithfulness, gentleness and self-control are the authenticating marks of Christianity that even a doubting world cannot overlook.

The following study of the Spirit's harvest in the ordinary believer's life is both basic and simple, and I hope that it will also be readable.

The world needs to see, and God longs to see the fruit of the Spirit in the life of every believer today. If that sounds like heaven on earth, then let us begin the process by making our cry *down with heaven!*

Ian Barclay

The fruit of the Spirit is love
Galatians 5.22

The eleventh commandment

Samuel Rutherford was the minister of the parish church at Anwoth in the early 17th century. His ministry was so effective and widely known that when Archbishop Usher passed through Galloway he wanted to hear Rutherford. The Archbishop decided not to arrive dressed as a clergyman, so he changed into the clothes of an ordinary traveller. At Anwoth he was immediately welcomed into the minister's house. Before the household retired to bed everybody gathered for teaching and prayer. Samuel Rutherford asked the stranger how many commandments there were. The disguised traveller replied, 'Eleven.' The minister of Anwoth corrected him, but the stranger insisted that he was right, and quoted the words of Jesus (in John 13.34) in support of his argument.

The next morning was Sunday, and Samuel Rutherford was up early and out for his usual walk through the woods. In a quiet clearing he found the traveller at prayer, asking God for the greatest possible blessing upon the whole of Anwoth that day. Samuel Rutherford realized that without his knowledge he had been entertaining a spiritual leader in his home; with the explanations over, the Archbishop agreed to preach at the morning service, and he took as his theme the eleventh commandment with the text, 'A new commandment I give to you.'

The new commandment sums up the New Testament's emphasis on holy living, and therefore it is not surprising that we find love as the first aspect of the fruit of the Spirit. The first quality that the Holy Spirit will bring into our lives is the ability to love in a new way.

Men without chests

When the writers of the New Testament looked out on the world of their day they saw men who talked about love, but who seemed to know little or nothing about the sort of love that the Holy Spirit was revealing to them. Their world was full of what C. S. Lewis called 'men without chests' – that is, men with a heartless love. So when the early Christians wanted to write about love they needed a new word. The Greek words in general use were not adequate: one word had too many sexual connotations, another meant merely natural affection and the third meant brotherly love. There was a verb that people had occasionally used, but no noun. So the New Testament writers took the verb and created a noun to describe this new love; a love that they did not want people ever to confuse with the sexual love, or the natural emotions that the other words implied.

A stranger to this planet

The love that the New Testament writers had in mind is a stranger to this planet. Indeed, John implies this in his first letter: 'See what love the Father has given us' – 'what *manner* of love' in AV (1 John 3.1). The word *manner* is not kept in many modern translations, but it is interesting that one of the original meanings of the Greek word can describe a foreign visitor. The love the Holy Spirit causes to flower in the Christian life is a love that is not naturally resident there; it is a total foreigner to this world.

It really could not be otherwise, because we are dealing with a supernatural love; a love that is 'poured into our hearts by the Holy Spirit.'

That isn't a friend, it is an enemy!

Man's natural love is centred on himself; when he finds something attractive, he loves it and wants it. Supernatural love has quite a different emphasis. It has the ability to love the unlovely and the unattractive. We see this quality in the way God loved us, because he loved us while we were still his enemies, while we were physically, spiritually and morally unattractive to him. Once the Holy Spirit begins to reveal this love to us, we too can begin to love our enemies.

A love that gives

A further quality of supernatural love is that it gives rather than demands. We see this again in the love that God has for us. John tells us that God 'so loved the world that he gave . . . '. And that we delight to give, rather than receive, will be a sign that the Holy Spirit is bringing this love into our lives.

Just outside the city of Sinope in the fourth century there lived a Christian called Phocas. Travellers frequently passed his gate, and he would persuade them to come into his garden and rest, so that they would go into the city refreshed. At the same time, he looked for every opportunity to share his faith with the travellers.

During the rule of the Emperor Diocletian, an order was issued that all Christians were to be put to death, and the name of Phocas of Sinope was high on the list issued by the magistrates. When the officers of the magistrates arrived at Sinope, hot and weary from a long day's journey, they did not need too much encouragement to turn aside into the garden of Phocas for refreshment. Phocas asked them their business in the area. The Commanding Officer said that they had orders from Rome to execute a local Christian called Phocas, and he went on to enquire of his whereabouts.

'I know him well', said Phocas. 'He doesn't live far away at all. Why don't you and your men rest for the night, and I will direct you to him in the morning.'

So the men from Rome retired for the night while Phocas went out into the garden that he loved so much. By the first light of morning he had dug a hole large enough to take a human body. At dawn he woke the Roman soldiers and told them he was Phocas. Bishop Asterious, who tells the story for us, recounts the astonishment of the men and their insistence that they could not put to death a man who had been so kind to them.

'Oh, please do,' said Phocas. 'I am a Christian, death is not important to me; whereas if you do not fulfil your orders you will get into trouble. Think of yourselves. You must do your duty. It will not alter my love and affection for you.'

So the execution took place, and the body was gently lowered into the garden grave. A love that had given so much to passing travellers had no more to give; it had given all.

The deep waters of hatred

It is a strange fact, but nontheless true, that Christians have sometimes been so convinced of the truth of their message that they have actually denied it by the way that they have lived. The Headmaster at Eton, when the poet Shelley was there, used to say to the boys, 'Be charitable, or I will flog you till you are.'

At the time of the Inquisition, the Spaniards captured an Inca chief in Central America. He knew that many of his people had been tortured by rack and thumb-screw into accepting the Christian faith. His captors asked him to become a Christian, assuring him of heaven if he did, but threatening him with immediate death and hell if he did not. He replied, 'I won't become a Christian. I would rather go to hell with my people than go to heaven with people like you.'

Many of our non-Christian friends would echo the reply of the Inca chief, simply because our lives are not consistent with what we say.

True love consists in loving my neighbour whoever he is, and in defending his life and property no matter how opposed he is to the Christian faith; to do otherwise is to stop loving, and to enter the mud and the 'deep waters of hatred' (Moffat's translation of Psalm 69.14).

Love does what friction cannot do

The greatest area of need for supernatural love is within the church. The church's failure to love dissipates her spiritual energy. R. G. LeTourneau, who invented the large earth-moving equipment used all over the world, commented that the mechanic's chief enemy is friction, and that friction could easily destroy over half of a machine's power. As a Christian he would often say that if friction causes wear in a machine, then it causes more damage in the human race.

You can see an example of the negative action of friction if you go into an unheated room in the middle of winter, where the windows have iced up on the inside. If you try to rub the ice away you will find that the harder you rub the faster the ice reforms. Turn on the fires in the room and the ice will soon melt away.

Therefore friction not only dissipates the church's power, it also hardens the spirit of coldness that destroys the church's life. A little warm-hearted supernatural love can melt even the spiritually coldest church. As Augustine said, 'One loving spirit sets another on fire.'

Journey of a lifetime

We have already seen that the love which the Holy Spirit brings into our lives is a stranger to the natural human heart. Therefore we cannot create this love; but we can create the conditions in which it will flourish.

D. L. Moody once remarked that 'some men occasionally take a journey into 1 Corinthians 13,' and I take it that he was implying that very few people actually live there. So let us take the journey into that part of 1 Corinthians 13 which deals with our relationship with other people. If we can begin to understand some of the things that the Holy Spirit brings into our lives through love, then perhaps we can concentrate on creating the conditions that will enable them to grow.

1 Love is not irritable (verse 5). I like these words because they are a reminder of how human the spiritual giants of a past age were. This truth was a bit too strong for the translators of the King James Version, so they translated it, 'Love is not easily provoked.' But by no stretch of the imagination can you find the word 'easily' in the text. We create the right environment for love by never being irritable. As someone said, 'If I ever get rubbed up the wrong way I immediately know that I am at fault, because I shouldn't have a wrong way to get rubbed up!'

2 Love is not resentful (verse 5). The word for 'resentful' is an accounting term, meaning that we must not add up and itemize the failures of other people. There is a story of a young American

2

student who went on his knees to God and confessed a particular sin, and promised never to do it again. Within an hour he was back on his knees, saying, 'O God, I have done it again.' A deep voice boomed from heaven, 'Done what?' God's forgiving love is so perfect that he forgives and forgets. And an equal forgetfulness in us about the failures of others is the only ground in which love grows.

3 *Love does not rejoice at wrong* (verse 6). It was always said of Archbishop Cranmer that if you did him a disfavour you had him as a friend for life. Certainly just before his martyrdom he said, 'I never had greater pleasure in all my life than to forget and forgive injuries and to show kindness to them that sought evil to me.'

4 *Love bears all things* (verse 7). The word 'bears' means to throw a cloak of silence over. The artist who was engaged to paint the portrait of Alexander the Great made the shadow of Alexander's hand conceal a scar on his brow. Love will flourish in a life that is not constantly drawing attention to the faults of others.

To embark on living that is not irritable, resentful, does not rejoice at wrong, is to begin the journey of a lifetime in living out the eleventh commandment.

The fruit of the Spirit is . . . joy
Galatians 5.22

Him serve with mirth

I can still remember my surprise when I first noticed the third line of the hymn *All people that on earth do dwell*. In my hymn book the words quite clearly said *Him serve with mirth*. My surprise was so great that I did not sing the rest of the hymn, but just stood there looking at the words. I had recently become a Christian and knew that many things in my life would have to change. I had presumed that the happy things like laughter and joy would be among the first to receive drastic alterations. I was too young a Christian to have heard the words of C. S. Lewis that 'joy is the serious business of heaven.'

The serious business of heaven

Joy is right at the heart of Christian truth, and so it should be right at the centre of experience too. There is no part of the Christian life that cannot be made more alive by joy, just as there are no circumstances, no matter how dark, which cannot be lightened by joy. The word *joy* that occurs in the list of the fruit of the Spirit also appears in 60 other places in the New Testament, while the associated word *to rejoice* occurs 72 times. And this is only one of the three New Testament words that mean *joy*, quite apart from the six from the Old Testament. All these have basically the same meaning, so it is not wrong to base our study on one from the Old Testament. In fact it is Nehemiah who gives us one of the most helpful studies of this word. He says:

'And they offered great sacrifices that day and rejoiced, for God had made them rejoice with great joy; the women and children also rejoiced. And the joy of Jerusalem was heard afar off' (Nehemiah 12.43).

In this verse we see the essential characteristic of biblical joy; that it is *great* joy. As with the sort of joy spoken of in this passage, not one of the Bible words for joy is in any sense a weak word. All of them describe a vividly exciting, exalting and exuberating experience. It is an experience that is so beyond description that Peter calls it 'unutterable joy' (1 Peter 1.8). It is such a light-headed experience that C. T. Studd, one of the pioneer missionaries of the last century, called it *delirium gaudens*, a 'deliriousness of rejoicing.'

It is certainly true that we have lost this joy from Christian living today. When people look at the Church they do not often see people who are full of joy. More often they see, to use Ernest Gordon's phrase, people who have managed to 'extract the bubbles from the champagne of life.' No wonder in his book *Miracles on the River Kwai* he says that before his conversion he 'preferred a robust hell to this grey, sunless abode of the faithful.' However, the experience of the faithful is not meant to be either grey or sunless. Joy can come into the life of a believer in several ways.

Good, merry, glad and joyful
First, there is clearly joy in believing. Time and again in the gospels we see people who become joyful as they meet Jesus Christ. There is nothing to suggest that the unscrupulous tax-collecting Zacchaeus was a happy man before he met Jesus, but after the meeting he welcomed Jesus into his home *joyfully* (Luke 19.6). The Ethiopian eunuch was confused by reading the Old Testament until Philip explained it to him. Philip's teaching led to the Ethiopian being baptized, and then he went on his way *rejoicing* (Acts 8.39).

To meet with Jesus is such a joyful experience that in the 16th century William Tynedale described the Christian gospel as 'good, merry, glad and joyfull tydings, that maketh a mannes hert glad, and maketh hym singe, dance and leepe for joy.'

It is remarkable how often the word *joy* is used as a summary of all that people feel at their conversion. C. S. Lewis called his autobiography *Surprised by Joy*. In it he told the story of his life as it moved from complete disbelief to the place where he found the reality of Jesus and, at the same time, joy.

The keen mind of Blaise Pascal made a similar discovery during the evening of the 23rd November 1654. Two hours later he tried to put his experience down on paper. It included the words 'joy,

joy, joy, tears of joy.' The words that Blaise Pascal wrote that night, he kept for the rest of his life on a piece of paper hidden in the lining of one of his coats. Before his conversion he had been a solemn person who disliked the 'follies and amusements of the world.' After his conversion he was so completely changed that his sister was shocked by his 'effervescence.'

Wild joys of living

Secondly, there is joy in Christian living. When Jesus defined the Christian life at the beginning of the Sermon on the Mount, he began each statement with the words, 'blessed . . . ' Jesus was not looking forward to something in the future but was speaking about a possible experience for his disciples in the present. It is almost impossible to translate into modern language all that Jesus meant by the word *blessed*, but it is certainly not less than knowing the joy of paradise on earth.

So it was not only the poet Robert Browning who spoke of the 'wild joys of living': it was also something Jesus offered his disciples. And it seems that the early Christians did in fact experience a wild joy in the face of all kinds of difficulties. Not only did they encourage others to be joyful when they were overtaken by hardships and trials (James 1.2), but when the same suffering came their own way they rejoiced 'that they were counted worthy to suffer' (Acts 5.41).

The normal greeting of New Testament times, used when two friends met or wrote a letter, came from the same word that Paul used for *joy* in

Galatians. Although it is normally translated as 'Greetings', to be strictly accurate it should read 'Joy be with you.' The letter James addressed to Christians scattered across the whole of the ancient world is the earliest part of the New Testament. As James begins with the normal greeting, you could say that the New Testament begins with the exclamation, 'Joy be with you!' It was certainly this message that the rest of the New Testament would echo time and time again as it came to be written.

A crown of joy

Thirdly, there is joy in winning others. Paul calls his converts his *joy* and crown. Although most of us shrink from sharing our faith with others, if the person to whom we witness is interested there is an unbelievable thrill in leading them into a personal experience of Jesus Christ. As we have seen, this is understandable as there are strong links in the New Testament between joy and the gospel. When we lead people to Christ we are sharing in the joy of discovering that which was lost.

A cheerful heart is good medicine

There is a natural inclination that can make us feel that the bubbling joy of the New Testament will never be ours, simply because of our own particular difficulties. This sort of reaction makes us feel that while our present problems remain we shall never be mildly happy, let alone wildly joyful. This is one reason why the verse in Nehemiah (12.43) is such a helpful study, because the

people of Nehemiah's day rejoiced in spite of grea.
problems and extremely adverse circumstances.

Nehemiah had been appointed Governor of
Judah by the Persian king Artaxerxes I. When
Nehemiah arrived in Jersusalem he was dismayed
at the state of the city. A hundred years earlier
43,000 Jews had returned from exile in Persia,
but very little rebuilding had taken place in the
intervening time. The temple had been rebuilt,
but the walls, obviously important for the city's
protection, still lay in ruins. And the inhabitants
of Jerusalem had been so continually harassed by
marauders that they were now in a state of
depressed inactivity.

After a night of reconnaissance, Nehemiah
persuaded the majority of the Israelites to help him
rebuild the walls. They worked under the
constant threat of attack from their enemies, and
in spite of continual grumblings from the Israelites
the walls were completely rebuilt in just over
seven weeks.

For the rededication of the wall the people
gathered at the Valley Gate, where they split
into two groups and proceeded to march around
the wall in opposite directions. When the two
groups met they swept through another gate into
the city and converged on the temple. It was when
the people arrived at the temple that they 'offered
great sacrifices that day and rejoiced.' With God's
help they had built the wall in the face of many
problems and difficulties, and although the problems were not over there was *great joy*.

Kingfisher days

It is not only in the historical books of the Bible that joy is much more likely to be produced by difficulty and hardship than by ease and relaxation. We are also told this by people who have had to pass through adversity. Sir Thomas More was not overwhelmed by the prospect of death as he went to the block in the year 1535; rather, he encouraged his wife to 'be merry in God.'

'Halcyon days' is a description that we sometimes use of an idyllic time on earth. *Halcyon* is simply the Greek word for a kingfisher. The phrase is based on a Greek legend about a kingfisher which lived in a golden age when the sea was so calm that it could actually build its nest on the waves and rear its young free from worry. Since the time of the Garden of Eden there has not been such a time on earth, and there is not likely to be one. Yet the bubbling joy of the Bible can be ours in spite of this. We can have joy without having 'Kingfisher days.'

However, many people continue to seek for the things that they feel will produce joy, so it is important for us to try and discover the ultimate source of joy. The easiest way to do this is first to list the things that cannot produce joy.

Firstly, joy does not come from happiness. Strictly speaking, happiness is not a biblical word at all. It comes from the root *to happen*: clearly what happens to us will affect our happiness. If we receive a letter tomorrow that informs us that a long-forgotten uncle has left us £10,000, there is a good chance that tomorrow we will be happy.

Equally, if tomorrow a doctor tells us that we will shortly die of cancer, presumably this will have a dampening effect on our happiness. Our happiness then changes with what happens to us. Joy is not altered by such changes, for it has a totally different source.

Secondly, joy does not come from our temperament. It was the Greek physician Hippocrates who around the turn of the third century BC first noted the differing temperaments of the individual members of the human race. Hippocrates distinguished four temperaments. Depending on the 'humours' of his body, a man's temperament would either be melancholic, choleric, phlegmatic or sanguine. No one has bettered these temperamental divisions of the human personality.

But a man's temperament does not make him joyful. For it was not only the easy-going sanguine Peter who knew joy (1 Peter 1.8); joy was also the experience of the choleric leader Paul (Philippians 4.4). Nor did joy escape the fearful, indecisively phlegmatic Abraham (Genesis 21.8); or even the moody melancholic Moses (Numbers 10.10). So if we are to discover the source of joy we must look outside the human personality, for the evidence of history is that in spite of our temperaments we can still be joyful.

Thirdly, joy does not come from sin. The Bible is an honest book and in a forthright way it speaks of the 'pleasures of sin' (Hebrews 11.24). There are undoubted physical and mental pleasures to be gained by sinning, even if the pleasurable experiences that they bring is short lived. But the lasting pleasure of joy cannot be found in sin.

We must be careful, however, not to say that anything pleasurable is necessarily sinful. 'Pleasure' is the word that we use to describe any agreeable experience that comes to us through our senses. And God 'richly furnishes us with everything to enjoy' (1 Timothy 6.17). So while we can enjoy things and experiences, they cannot bring us lasting joy in the deep sense of the word.

Where joy is to be found

The source of all joy is God. Joy does not depend on circumstances or on temperament, but is firmly rooted in God and in our relationship with him. Because he loves us and he never changes, there is a basic security underneath all the problems. This is the secret of joy. The verse in Nehemiah tells us that 'God made them rejoice with great joy.' And that is really what Paul is saying when he calls joy one of the fruits of the Spirit. When joy is seen in a man it is the evidence of God at work; therefore joy comes from him.

Let there be no silly talk and levity

There are Christians who shrink away from joy, gaiety and laughter because Paul said that they were not to engage in silly talk and levity (Ephesians 5.14). But the context shows that Paul was not talking about a good laugh but about *impure* talk and levity. J. S. Whale in his book *Christian Doctrine* says that one of the distinctive features of man is that he is a laughing animal. And this characteristic is just as much a part of man's spiritual nature as of his physical and mental make-up. Helmut Thielicke condemns those who would say otherwise:

'Should we not see that lines of laughter about the eyes are just as much marks of faith as are the lines of care and seriousness? Is it only earnestness that is baptized? Is laughter pagan? We have already allowed too much that is good to be lost to the church and cast many pearls before swine. A church is in a bad way when it banishes laughter from the sanctuary and leaves it to the cabaret, the night club and the toastmasters.'

Easter laughter

The last thing that we must notice about joy is that it is contagious. In Nehemiah's day joy spread to those near at hand 'and the joy of Jerusalem was heard afar off.' Whenever joy appears in the church it spreads quickly. When the Spirit of God moved through Wheaton College in Illinois while Leighton Ford was there, the Principal remarked, 'We have never seen so many smiles per square face!'

At Easter time in the medieval church in the days before the liturgy was fixed, the minister would stand to read a passage from the Bible. Often the whole congregation would be so moved by the resurrection story that they quite spontaneously broke out in *the laughter of Easter*. Such contagious joy would have a tremendous effect if only it would break out in the church today. We desperately need the laughter of Easter.

The fruit of the Spirit is . . . peace
Galatians 5.22

An instrument of thy peace

It is Francis of Assisi who takes us right to the heart of the matter so far as peace is concerned, for he prayed, 'Make me an instrument of thy peace.' This is a reminder that Christianity is not merely about being at peace, but is also about becoming peacemakers. So, when we experience fully the aspect of the fruit of the Spirit that Paul calls 'peace', we must not expect to find ourselves in a quiet cul-de-sac, cut off from the harsh realities of life. It is much more likely that we will find ourselves in the most unpeaceful surroundings for the purposes of making peace. In such circumstances, we won't find it easy to be instruments of peace, but we should find that nothing can disturb our own peace. To be at peace, when there is no peace, sounds paradoxical, so perhaps we should discover what the Bible means by peace.

It is easier to say what it isn't!
First, it is not merely the absence of activity. Someone who works in a very busy office may often feel that he could do twice as much work if he did not have to put up with the noise of other

33

people and the telephone. Should the office suddenly empty and the telephone become unusually quiet, he might exclaim, 'What peace!'

But that is not what the Bible means by peace. Peace is more than the mere absence of activity. That is why you find Christians who are at peace while living the most hectic lives. A good example of this is Dr Paul Carlson, the missionary who was killed by rebels in the Congo in 1964. He had to care for over 100,000 patients. He saw hundreds of them each week and performed at least one major surgical operation every day. On the day before he was killed, in spite of being in the midst of a colossal amount of work, he wrote in his New Testament the single word 'peace.'

We can be at peace even when we are the centre of activity. If we can only discover a sense of quietness by escaping from activity, then what we have found is not the peace of the New Testament.

Secondly, it is not merely the absence of hostility. We may visit a home where there is so much disagreement and bickering that we long to get away to a more peaceful atmosphere. However, if we do get away the mere absence of strife won't create the peace of the New Testament. The peace that the Bible speaks about is something that can be experienced in spite of the most adverse and hostile conditions.

When the Indian Christian Sadhu Sundar Singh was arrested for preaching the gospel he was condemned to being left naked in the market place covered with leeches. The authorities thought that they would drive Sadhu Sundar Singh insane during the night, or even cause him to die of fright. However, he was very much alive in the morning and the authorities were amazed at his calmness. Speaking of the experience afterwards, he said that all the time he was conscious of 'an intense inward peace.'

Thirdly, peace is not merely the absence of reality. We all suffer occasionally from the irrational belief that if we could only escape from where we are, we could then find peace. The countryman thinks he can find peace in the changing scenery of a town, while the city dweller feels that if he could get away from the rush of the city he could find peace in the quietness of the countryside. Yet the offer of the Bible is that we can find peace right where we are, and there is no suggestion that we will ever find it by escaping from reality.

Edward FitzGerald, the translator of the Rubaiyat of Omar Khayam, thought that he could find peace if he exchanged his present life for his imaginary ideal life. So he left his wife, with whom he had been very unhappy, and went and lived in the country. He occupied himself with congenial work; he even kept doves, the birds of peace. But peace continued to elude him. New Testament peace is never found by getting away from reality. To find peace of mind we do not have to escape from what is, to what we would like to be.

A roaring, stirring, happy thing
Sometimes the word 'peace' is used in the Bible in exactly the same sense that we would use it

35

today; but it also has a special meaning. It means such spiritual satisfaction, physical well-being, mental tranquillity, that even the possibility of war, strife, and animosity can be completely forgotten. This kind of peace can be seen when the Spirit of God totally grips a man and then sweeps out through him to affect his environment as well. Peace in this sense is perfect harmony between God, man and nature. No wonder that Helmut Thielicke said that peace is 'not dull stagnation but is a soaring, stirring, happy thing.'

This idea of peace affecting every part of man's life can be seen in the variety of meanings of the Old Testament word. It is used for *absolute victory* (1 Kings 22.27), *physical health* (Psalm 38.3), *a friend* (Jeremiah 20.10), *the era when the Messiah reigns* (Isaiah 9.6), *prosperity* (Job 15.21), *welfare* (Genesis 43.27) and *a time of security and calm* (Judges 6.23, Isaiah 32.17). The New Testament writers injected this broad Hebrew meaning into the New Testament definition of the word peace, and it is the background of the word each time it occurs in the New Testament.

A walking civil war

Most people lack peace because they are a walking civil war. Any natural tranquillity that they might have is constantly being dissipated by inner conflict, which can spring from four basic conditions in a man's life.

Firstly, the restless spirit. It was Augustine, the North African fourth century bishop, who said, 'Restless is the heart until it finds rest in thee.'

Modern man is seen trying to dull his restless spirit with everything from sexual experience to filling his day with sounds. It is this same restless spirit that makes people work from the moment they get up until they go to bed. It is not that they have to fill each day with activity, so much as that they must escape the nagging restlessness that only God can satisfy.

Secondly, the guilty conscience. The guilty conscience is similar to the restless heart, in that there is no man-made medicine that can offer relief or cure.

This is nowhere better illustrated than in the life of the 16th century reformer, Thomas Bilney. While he was at Cambridge University in 1519 he tried everything in his search for peace. Even the continual round of confession and sacrament that the priests had suggested all failed to heal his guilty conscience. He put it like this, 'My soul was sick and I longed for peace, but nowhere could I find it.'

The answer came in the form of the New Testament, newly translated into Latin and published on the continent by Erasmus. After reading it, Thomas Bilney said, 'I chanced upon these words, "This is a faithful saying and worthy of all acceptation, that Christ Jesus came into the world to save sinners." That one saying so lifted up my bruised spirit that it was as if, after a dark night, day suddenly broke.' Only the forgiveness that Jesus offers can still and quieten a guilty conscience.

Thirdly, the lonely heart. Simply to state the

phrase makes it sound like the title of a television situation comedy, whereas one of the hard facts of a fallen world is that everybody is essentially alone. It is not just the elderly or the single, or even people who live in cities, who are lonely; it is a fact of life for all.

It ought not to be so, but one of the results of the fall is that when man cut himself off from God, he also cut himself off from his fellows. The more a society moves away from God, the more fragmented it becomes, and consequently the more isolated individual men feel. Loneliness can be hidden for a time, just as for a time it can be forgotten; but only in restoring a relationship with God, and through him with our fellow men, can it be removed. Loneliness is one of the basic reasons for disquiet in the human race.

Fourthly, the troubled mind. The last reason for this inner conflict is fear. As I write, one of the more famous television dance groups is called *Pan's People*, and it is easy to look at them and think that to be totally abandoned and natural is the secret of inner peace.

But this could hardly be further from the truth. Our word 'panic' comes from the name of the Greek god Pan. Pan's people are frightened people. For it is not being away from the pressures of life, but being away from God, that makes a man frightened. When a new tribe is discovered deep in the equatorial jungle, their lives are more often marked by fear than peace. Panic, terror, 'nerves' are all part of the consequences of living in a fallen world.

A quiet people in a bad world

An old Chinese proverb sums this up well when it says, 'He who is not at peace with heaven cannot be at peace with himself; therefore he will never be at peace with his neighbour.' The special peace of the Bible can only begin to be found when we have peace with God.

So, in spite of the fact that the consequences of the fall vastly reduce the chance of man ever finding peace, the secret of true tranquillity can be found. A third century Christian put it like this in a letter to a friend:

'It is a bad world, Donatus, an incredibly bad world. But I have discovered in the midst of it a quiet and holy people who have learnt a great secret. They have found a joy which is a thousand times better than any of the pleasures of our sinful life. They are despised and persecuted, but they care not. They are masters of their souls. They have overcome the world. These people, Donatus, are Christians, and I am one of them.'

The quiet people in a bad world are those who have accepted Christ. New birth means that a man's guilt is removed, his restlessness has gone, and the reason for his innate fear and loneliness are removed.

Christians are still living in the fallen world, and will still suffer the consequences of the fall, such as pain and disease. To have peace does not mean necessarily that we will never experience the disturbed emotions which accompany these things. It is at a deeper level than that: we have peace with God through Christ. As the old hymn puts it,

'The clouds may go and come, and storms may sweep my sky', but our relationship with God remains secure. To have Christ means to have such certain peace that the New Testament says it 'garrisons' a man's heart and mind (Philippians 4.7).

A wilderness called peace

As the conditions of a man's conscience and his mind and heart can easily affect the whole of his personality, it should not surprise us that these are easy targets for the attacks of the devil. We must therefore expect the devil to try constantly to undermine the peace of mind of the believer.

One of the ways in which he does this is by making us feel guilty when we become upset or despondent. 'Where is your peace now?' he jeers at us. We can best combat him not by accusing ourselves, nor by trying to 'work up' a peaceful feeling; but by reminding ourselves of the roots of our peace in Christ and what he has done, and strengthening our relationship with him.

The last will and testament

Jesus must have known that special difficulties would confront his disciples so far as this particular fruit of the Spirit was concerned, because he was careful to leave them the legacy of peace. Just before his death he said, 'My peace I leave you.' Matthew Henry said, 'When Christ died he left a will, in which he bequeathed his soul to his Father, his body to Joseph of Arimathea, his clothes fell to the soldiers, his mother he gave to John, but to his disciples, who had left all for him, he left not silver and gold but something that was infinitely better – his peace.'

So peace is our inheritance: we have it by right.

The fruit of the Spirit is . . . patience
Galatians 5.22

The queen of virtues

There are two words in the New Testament that are translated into English as 'patience.' John Chrysostom described one of them as 'the queen of virtues, the foundation of right action, peace in war, calm in tempest, security in plots,' and this is a good description of both kinds of New Testament patience.

In the New Testament, patience is a complex word. When Miles Coverdale translated the Bible into English in 1535 he had to invent the word 'longsuffering' to describe the word that he found in Galatians 5. It was such a good, literal translation of the New Testament word that the translators of the Authorised Version in 1611 kept it. What Miles Coverdale was trying to express was that in contrast to the person who is short-tempered, the Christian's life must be marked by long-temper.

Patience in this sense is a 'spiritual' word. It is not found in the ordinary literature outside the New Testament, yet it does have a history that stretches back long before the New Testament was written. Right through the Old Testament we find the idea that God is merciful and gracious, and 'slow to anger' (Exodus 34.6, Nehemiah 9.17, Psalm 86.15, 145.8). The phrase 'slow to anger' in the Greek version of the Old Testament is the single word 'patience' or 'long-suffering' or, quite literally, 'long-temperedness.' So we are here dealing with something which is at the heart of God's nature, as well as something which ought to be seen in every Christian life.

You can afford to wait

In the sense that it can be seen in the Christian life, patience has four basic meanings:

Firstly, it means long-lasting patience. It was Thomas Carlyle who said, 'If you have a creed you can afford to wait.' And this is nowhere better demonstrated than in his own life.

He had been working on his book *The French Revolution* for some time, and when the first volume was finished Carlyle took the manuscript to his friend John Stuart Mill for comment and advice. Mill loaned it to a Mrs Chapman who read it by the fire on the evening of March 5, 1834, and left it on the mantelpiece when she went to bed. Long before she was up the next morning her servants dusted her sitting room and relit the fire. A servant girl thought that 'the papers' on the mantelpiece would make an excellent fire-lighter. In a few minutes the work of months was lost. But such was the long-lasting patience of Thomas Carlyle that he immediately began the task of writing the manuscript again.

There is a similar story told of Sir Isaac Newton

who spent eight years preparing a major work. When he entered his study one morning he discovered that his pet dog, Diamond, had knocked over a candle that had completely destroyed the papers on his desk. Without any sign of anger or impatience Sir Isaac Newton quietly remarked to his dog, 'Diamond, little do you know the labour and trouble to which you have put your master!' And he sat down at his desk to start the vast work again.

While long-lasting patience is concerned with events and circumstances, it is supremely linked with our attitude towards other people. A missionary from Ethiopia told a marvellous story about an African woman who became increasingly impatient with her husband. Married life became so strained that she went to her doctor for something to make her husband love her more. The doctor replied that such a prescription wasn't easy to make as husbands were notoriously difficult to treat. He said that he would need the woman's help in gathering the basic ingredients for such powerful medicine, and firstly he would require 'three hairs from the mane of a live lion.'

The lady went home wondering how she would be able to get the necessary material for the medicine. When she heard that a lion was prowling near a local village she took the largest goat from her herd and tied it to a tree hoping to tempt the lion. Sure enough, the lion came and took the goat. The next day the lady tied another goat to the tree, and the process went on for several weeks until the whole herd had been used as bait.

Each day the lady had managed to get a little nearer to the lion and on the final day even managed to talk to him. She said, 'I am sorry to trouble you, but I wonder if I could have three hairs from your mane?' 'Of course,' replied the lion. 'Take what you wish; after all, I have enjoyed your goats.'

The next day the ingredients were taken triumphantly to the doctor. And he said, 'You must have been extremely patient to get these hairs from the mane of a living lion. Now go home and put the same amount of patience into your marriage!'

More than anything else, the Christian must show a long-lasting patience to other people.

Blessed adversity

Secondly, it means long-lasting endurance. The New Testament scholar Alfred Plummer defined this word as 'forbearance which endures injuries and evil deeds without being provoked to anger or revenge.' It would be easy to think that we are dealing with good old-fashioned resignation; but that is not true. Patience does not merely accept life with resignation, but also reacts to it in a positive, creative way.

If John Bunyan had merely been resigned to his unjust imprisonment, presumably he would have been a model prisoner for 13 years. However, he wasn't merely a good prisoner: he also used the time to create *Pilgrim's Progress*, one of the spiritual masterpieces of all time. To a lesser degree, there was creative endurance in the life of the young Ralph Vaughan Williams when he was told not to continue his music studies because he was so bad at them. And the same characteristic is seen in the life of the future Lord Montgomery when he was told at Sandhurst that because he was so bad at military procedure he would get nowhere in the Army. Fortunately for history, both these men had the long-lasting endurance that proved their teachers wrong.

There is a delightful memorial to a man who lived in the Cotswolds in the 16th century. It reads, 'Drive out fear from my heart, O my body. I believe that you shall appear before God in Christ; for he it is that sustains you and calls you to dwell with him. Laugh at the threats of disease, despise the blows of misfortune, care not for the dark grave and go forward at Christ's summons.' It is long-lasting endurance which despises the blows of misfortune.

Not summer soldiers
Thirdly, it means long-lasting courage. Tom Paine coined the phrase 'summer soldiers' to describe the soldiers of Washington who had lost their courage. It was in the year 1776 when the American troops were in a bad way because of the lack of food and shortage of ammunition. Their shabby clothing and a long series of defeats made them feel that their final collapse was inevitable. However, Tom Paine inspired them to victory with a pamphlet entitled *The Crisis*, which began with the words, 'These are times that try men's souls. The summer soldier and the sunshine

patriot will, in this crisis, shrink from the service of his country.' Patience ensures that the Christian is not merely a summer soldier, for it adds long-lasting courage to endurance. Dr W. E. Sangster used to tell a story of something that his father had actually seen at the time the Salvation Army began. People everywhere were opposed to William Booth's new spiritual army. They even enlisted in a force called the Skeleton Army for the sole purpose of opposing the work of William Booth's young men and women.

Outside the 'Eagle Tavern' in the City Road, London, a young Salvation Army officer was preaching to a tiny crowd when a very drunk man came out. The drunk hit the preacher so hard that he fell and hit his head with a loud thud on the curb. The sound of the fall and the way that the preacher lay still quickly sobered the man. Eventually the young Salvationist got up; he still looked dazed but he managed to smile and say to the man who had hit him, 'May God bless you, sir.' And he began preaching where he had left off. Patience gives the Christian a long-lasting courage.

With malice towards none
Lastly, it means long-lasting forgiveness. One of the most remarkable men that I have ever met was Donald Caskie, the minister of the Scottish church in Paris, who told his fascinating story in *The Tartan Pimpernel*. In 1940 he had to flee from his church to the South of France, where he exchanged his clerical collar for the cloak and

dagger of the French Resistance. Eventually he was caught and imprisoned in some of the most fearful prisons of the Second World War, including the Villa Lynwood where he saw Odette Churchill.

Donald Caskie survived the privation and tortures of imprisonment to return to Paris in August 1944. When he first unlocked his church which had been closed for four years, the key was stiff in the lock and the dust lay thickly throughout the whole building. As he knelt to thank God for his deliverance he was determined to make the words of Abraham Lincoln his guide in the days to come:

'With malice towards none, with charity for
   all;
With firmness in the right as God gives me
   to see it;
Let us strive on to finish the work we are in;
To bind up the nation's wounds.'

When regret or even bitterness seems the most natural reaction for a man, it is patience that enables him to regard his persecutors without malice.

Masterpieces take time
Mona Lisa's famous smile took Leonardo da Vinci four years to paint. And the masterpiece of a truly patient life is going to take some time to produce. That is why the call to be patient in every circumstance of life comes repeatedly in the Bible. The Christian is to 'put on patience' (Colossians 3.12), and he is to 'walk . . . with

patience' (Ephesians 4.2 AV). Even while suffering 'calamities, beatings, imprisonment, tumults ... hunger' he is to be patient (2 Corinthians 6.5-6). Indeed, when such trying experiences are accepted patiently, they will produce joy (Colossians 1.11, Hebrews 12.2), for it is patient endurance that enables the Christian to obtain the promise of God (Hebrews 6.15).

How can I find patience?

A young man once went to his pastor, George Muller, with a spiritual problem. He said, 'Mr Muller, my Christian life lacks patience. I wonder if you could show me how to find it?'

George Muller told the young man that his problem wasn't too difficult to solve, and suggested that they both knelt in prayer. The pastor prayed, 'Lord, I want you to give this young man some tribulation in his life. Give him weeks of tribulation; make that the experience of every moment of every day.'

The young man got up and pulled George Muller to his feet. 'I am sorry, I think that you must have misunderstood me – it is patience that I want, not tribulation.'

'Indeed,' said the pastor. 'The Bible quite clearly says that "tribulation worketh patience", so you won't find it in any other way.'

The fruit of the Spirit is . . . kindness
Galatians 5.22

My yoke is kind

If you want to study quartz you should not look at the rock from which it comes but at the crystals into which it is forming. The fruit of the Spirit could be called 'the crystallization of the spiritual life', and the particular aspect that we are going to look at in this chapter is kindness.

A possible clue
The phrase used by Jesus in one rather remarkable place possibly gives a clue to its practical meaning. In Matthew 11.30 Jesus says, 'My yoke is easy', and the word 'easy' is the New Testament word 'kind!'

In Bible times a farmer would take his ox to the carpenter to be fitted with a yoke. The carpenter, after taking measurements, would rough out the yoke before calling the farmer back with his ox to have it exactly fitted to the animal's back. Obviously the animal wouldn't be happy and efficient if the yoke chafed or caused irritation in any way.

Jesus followed the profession of Joseph his earthly father before he began his public ministry, and there is a legend that as a carpenter he made the best yokes in the whole of Galilee. Someone has suggested that the sign over his shop must have said, 'My yokes fit well.' We don't know the truth about that, but we do know that he said, 'My yoke is kind.'

This link between the word 'kindness' and the picture of the ox and its yoke helps to give us a clearer definition of the word.

Sweetness of temper
Firstly, kindness enables a man to fit smoothly into society. Jesus says, 'My yoke is kind'; it doesn't chafe or irritate in any way. The Holy Spirit brings into the life of a believer a quality that enables him to fit easily into society. Gone is the old bitter, antagonistic, censorious spirit-kindness now takes its place. A man's heart is filled with what Alfred Plummer calls a 'sweetness of temper which puts others at ease, and shrinks from giving pain.'

To see how this is done, we must discover why people are not naturally kind. The Chinese proverb already quoted states it well, 'He who is not at peace with heaven, cannot be at peace with himself, therefore will never be at peace with his neighbour.' Here is a sequence that we can follow.

The Villa Plague
The sequence begins by finding peace with God, because he is the only person who can change the human heart, and all bitterness and antagonism spring from the heart. As Jesus said, 'Out of the

heart come evil thoughts, murder, adultery, fornication, theft, false witness, slander' – just as Jeremiah had suggested years before, 'the heart is deceitful above all things and desperately corrupt.'

Not long ago we decided to take a few days' holiday at the seaside. We had told the children where we were staying but hadn't actually told them the name of the hotel. As our car swung into the drive, the beam of the headlights caught the hotel sign and Helen exclaimed, 'We're going to stay at a hotel called the Villa Plague!' My wife explained that the hotel was called the *Villa Plage* which simply meant *House by the Sea*. During our few days' holiday I was reading 1 Kings 8.38 (AV) which speaks of every man knowing 'the plague of his own heart.' Man's heart is indeed a Hotel of Plagues.

Dr Christiaan Barnard in South Africa was the first man successfully to perform a heart transplant operation. One day he was talking to Philip Blaiberg, and asked him if he would like to see his heart. When the patient said 'yes,' a glass container was lifted from a shelf and handed to him. A few moments' silence followed as the first man in history actually gazed at his own heart. Then the two men talked about it. Finally Philip Blaiberg said, 'So that is the old heart that caused me so much trouble,' and he handed it back, turned away and left it for ever.

We can do the same; we can turn our back on our old heart because God has said, 'A new heart I will give you, and a new spirit I will put within you' (Ezekiel 36.26).

At peace with ourselves

The second step in the sequence is finding peace with ourselves, and once we have a new heart it is possible to find such peace. Dr Paul Rees tells of a lady who so lacked personal peace that she desired to dominate her whole family. Even though she was crippled with arthritis nothing stopped this desire. But having found peace with God, she realized the self-centredness of her behaviour and surrendered it to God; immediately her arthritis left her. Obviously not all arthritis is caused by selfishness, but all selfishness is crippling in some way. If we have peace with God we can also be at peace with ourselves and therefore the crippling effect of self-centredness can be taken away.

Old and mellow

When there is peace with God and we are at peace with ourselves, we will be at peace with our neighbour: it is as inevitable as that. Of course, this does not mean that our neighbour will always want to be at peace with us: that should not affect our attitude to him.

In Luke 5.39 the word 'kind' is used of a wine that has grown old and mellow. Kindness banishes the harshness and bitterness from the human heart until, like an old wine, it is smooth and mellow. 'Sweetness' is the way the Rheims version translates 'kindness' in 2 Corinthians 6.6. So kindness enables us to fit easily into society.

The road of the loving heart

Secondly, kindness enables a man to fit service into society. 'My yoke is kind,' said Jesus. No matter how well fitting, a yoke declares an animal to be a serving beast. Kindness will certainly make a man mellow, but it won't make him soft. When the Holy Spirit brings kindness into a man's life it will move him into service, so that even the community in which he lives will notice it.

Robert Louis Stevenson was very unwell while staying on Samoa, but he continued to show great kindness to the islanders. His condition worsened, and he was confined to sitting on the porch of his hut, from which he could only see the dark trees of the jungle. One day he was surprised to see the forest suddenly filled with half-naked savages cutting the trees down. They had heard that Stevenson wanted to see the breakers rolling on to the beach, and because they were so grateful for the many kindnesses he had shown them, they had come to cut a clearway from his hut to the beach. Stevenson wanted to pay them, but they refused, asking only that they might be allowed to name the pathway through the trees. They called it 'The Road of a Loving Heart.' Every Christian should so serve his community that his neighbours will want to change the name of his road in a similar way!

One brief hour before sunset

If kindness is so practical that it makes us serve the community, it also demands surrender in three basic areas of Christian living.

(*a*) *It will mean the surrender of our time.* There are two words in the New Testament for time. The first simply means 'a period of time' or 'the duration of time,' and the second means 'critical time' or 'opportunity.' In Ephesians 5.16 where Paul speaks of 'making the most of time,' the word that he uses is concerned with 'critical time.' For Christian people all time is critical. That is why Robert Moffat said, 'We will have all eternity to celebrate our victories, but only one brief hour before sunset to win them.'

(*b*) *It will mean the surrender of our talents.* Peter Claver was born in Verdu in Spain in the year 1581. His parents were very rich and of impeccable ancestry. When he left college in Barcelona his family wanted him to go into the church; his natural ability and family connections would have meant that he would have risen quickly to high office in that profession. But instead Peter Claver went to Cartagena in the West Indies to help the occupants of the slave ships as they arrived from Africa.

When a slave ship was sighted, the quayside would clear, for even the strongest of men could hardly bear the sight, let alone the smell. Hundreds of men and women had been chained together, unable to move, during the long sea voyage; some had died, some were dying, many were ill, all were desperately unclean.

Peter Claver surrendered the natural talents that he had and gave his life to meeting slave ships and going on board to care for the living and bury the dead. No wonder Goethe said, 'kindness is the golden chain by which society is joined together.'

(*c*) *It will mean the surrender of our treasure.* There is a story told of a circus athlete who performed astonishing feats of strength. He would conclude his performance by squeezing an orange until every drop of juice was crushed from the fruit. Sometimes he would issue a challenge to his audience to produce someone who could equal the amount of juice he had pressed from the orange.

On one occasion the crowd was extremely astonished when a very tiny man accepted the challenge. He slowly took the orange in his hands and squeezed until he had produced twice as much juice as the professional performer. When the cheering had subsided, someone asked him how it was done. 'Oh, it's easy,' he said. 'I'm the treasurer of the local church.'

Sadly, it is so often true that pressure needs to be applied before Christians will give. Kindness enables us to surrender our time, our talents and out treasure, *without pressure*, to the service of the community.

All this world needs

Thirdly, kindness enables a man to fit sovereignty into society. Jesus said, 'my yoke is kind.' The yoke we wear shows us to be those who serve, but it also declares who our master is. Putting on kindness shows us to be 'God's chosen ones' (Colossians 3.12), and without that declaration we are not living out the kindness of the New Testament. Because she suggested otherwise, Ella Wheeler Wilcox was wrong when she said,

'So many gods, so many creeds,
So many paths that wind and wind,
While just the art of being kind
Is all the sad world needs.'

Our society needs men and women who are filled with kindness because they are willing to declare quite openly that Jesus is their master.

The brief span of a believer's time on earth must be motivated by a kindness that will enable him to take Jesus into his society against all opposition to do otherwise.

Kindness is irresistible

George Sweeting, the minister of Chicago's famous Moody Church, tells of a pastor in Pennsylvania who had discovered two rather lonely ladies living in a dilapidated house, so he sent one of his church members to call. She walked down an untidy garden path to a little-used front door opened by two frightened ladies. The inside of the house was in a terrible state, and the two old ladies obviously hadn't left it for years, being terrified at the violence of the outside world. Although the ladies were so dirty and unkempt, the church visitor felt she had to hug them and say, 'God loves you, and so do I.'

Soon other church families were calling with provisions and helping to springclean the house. Friendships began to develop which included a rather timid time of prayer. Eventually the ladies made a decision to receive Christ. By then their house was tidy and they were changed to ordinary neatly-dressed citizens of the town. George Sweeting in recounting the story says that kindness implies active service, and goes on to say, 'What an evidence of the indwelling presence of Christ we can present when we express to others the warm loving-kindness that is characteristic of our Saviour.' There is no wonder the ladies found Christ. As Marcus Aurelius said, 'Kindness is irresistible, when it is sincere and no mock smile or mask assumed.'

Being cruel to be kind

There is a story about a man called Pambo who went to a wise man to be taught a psalm. The wise man thought that psalm 39 would be a good place to begin, so he said, 'Say after me, "I will guard my ways, that I may not sin with my tongue".'

Pambo repeated this line several times. When the wise man started to teach the next line Pambo said, 'Wait a minute, I'll be back to learn more, when I have really learned these words.'

Several months passed before they met again, but when asked if he was ready to learn more Pambo gave the same reply, and he was still giving it 40 years later.

Some people quote Hamlet and say that there are occasions when they need 'to be cruel to be kind.' Of course a Christian should never be deliberately cruel; whatever the excuse, it is always wrong. It is in any case going to take the Holy Spirit some time to teach us kindness, and we must make sure we have really learned that thoroughly.

The fruit of the Spirit is . . . goodness
Galatians 5.22

Too true to be good

Too true to be good is the title of a play by George Bernard Shaw. The playwright called the main character Private Meek; a part he obviously modelled on Lawrence of Arabia. Bernard Shaw saw Lawrence as being so idealistic that he had ceased to be attractive as a personality, and many would say that Christian goodness is so demanding that it makes life unattractive and dull.

Dr John Gossip of Scotland said, 'It is held by many, as the first axiom, that holiness is a dull affair, and God's company intolerably dreary, and that for vividness and colour and interest you must look elsewhere.'

Others would hold the reverse position and say that the ideals of the New Testament are far too good to be true; that what the New Testament offers is quite beyond belief and human experience. Of course, those whose lives are governed by the actions and attitudes of the world will see the fruit of the Spirit as totally beyond achievement. However, providing that the Holy Spirit occupies a human life, then there is no reason why that life cannot flower and bear fruit in a supernatural way.

A thousand unsuspected beauties

Goodness is a divine fact. A man came to Jesus and said, 'What good deed must I do, to have eternal life?' We are told by Matthew that Jesus replied, 'Why do you ask me about what is good? One there is who is good.' Jesus is quite clearly referring to God, and he describes him as being *good*. The basic meaning of goodness is a generosity that springs from a kind heart. The God whom Jesus describes as being absolutely good is not so morally correct that he is narrow and dull; rather he is so good that he actually litters the world with his attractiveness.

Dr Paul Rees speaks of Nansen's description of Arctic scenes and phenomena, particularly the Aurora Borealis, and goes on to say, 'You know that even the loneliest and remotest areas of this little planet, untrodden by man's foot, unadorned by his hand, hold, for those who respond to their strange allure, a thousand unsuspected beauties.'

We are not told of the Christian views of that famous fictional detective, Sherlock Holmes, but his perceptiveness brought him to the same conclusion as Dr Rees. Holding a rose in his hand, Holmes said, 'There is nothing in which deduction is so necessary as in religion. It can be built up as an exact science by the reasoner.

'Our highest assurance of the goodness of Providence seems to me to rest in the flowers. All other things, our desires, our food, are really necessary for our existence. But this rose is an extra. Its smell and its colour are an embellishment of life, not a condition of it. It is only goodness which gives extras, and so I say again that we have much hope from the flowers.'

I would not agree with Sherlock Holmes if he is saying that we only see the 'extras' of God's goodness in flowers, but they are certainly one of the unsuspected beauties of the world. Goodness is, then, a divine fact of the spiritual life, and that means that for every human being who is beginning to enjoy spiritual living, goodness also becomes a possibility.

A man full of goodness

To see what goodness in a human life is like, let us look at the life of Barnabas, whom Luke describes as 'a good man.' If we can discover the practical elements in the goodness of Barnabas, then perhaps we can begin to consider the spiritual possibilities that lie before us.

It is very important that we are exact in our practical definition of goodness, because as William Blake said, 'He who would do good to another must do it in minute particulars; general good is the plea of the scoundrel, hypocrite and flatterer.' The Barnabas of whom Luke wrote in the New Testament was good in minute particulars.

The first minute particular of the practical goodness of Barnabas was that for him property was not a matter of ownership but of stewardship.

We read that Barnabas 'sold a field which belonged to him, and brought the money and laid it at the apostles' feet' (Acts 4.37).

This statement stands in stark contrast to the story in the very next verse, where we read that

5

Ananias and Sapphira sold property and pretended to lay all the benefits of the sale at the apostles' feet. One of the ways that real goodness will be seen in us is the way that we give. We can measure it in ourselves by whether we regard ourselves to be the owners or simply the stewards of all that God has given to us. Others will see goodness in us by the way that we adjust our giving to a particular need, or by the way that we mould that need to our giving.

There is a delightful story of the hard-working secretary of J. M. Barrie who had not been to a first night of any of her employer's works. It had never occurred to Barrie to invite her, but a producer, who was aware that she wanted to be present, sent her two tickets for the stalls on an opening night. The secretary was thrilled, but in the end felt that she must return the tickets as she had nothing suitable to wear for such a special occasion. During one of the final rehearsals Barrie was informed of his secretary's dilemma. 'Oh, that is easy to solve', he said. 'I will change her tickets for two in the gallery.'

Barnabas gave; and that is one of the practical ways that goodness can be recognized. Giving must always be moulded by the need, not the other way around.

Perfect love casts out fear

The second minute particular of the practical goodness of Barnabas was that for him enemies did not provoke animosity but love. We read that just after Paul was converted he returned to

Jerusalem and wanted to join the disciples. The disciples were afraid of Paul because they were not absolutely convinced of the reality of his conversion. Then we are told, 'But Barnabas took him, and brought him to the apostles.'

Perfect love casts out fear and suspicion, and is willing to show love to both friends and enemies alike. The discerning goodness of Barnabas meant that his love went out to Paul across the barriers of opposition, and that in due course Paul was accepted by the other Christians.

Few people have exercised a greater ministry of love despite opposition than Thomas Boston, who was the minister of the little church at Ettrick in Selkirkshire, in a wild and desolate part of Scotland.

Thomas Boston arrived as minister of Ettrick on May Day, 1707, the day that England and Scotland were finally united under one crown. At first the people of Ettrick nearly broke the young minister's heart. There were few church members, and the majority of the people were so outwardly immoral and godless that they actually fought noisily in the churchyard during the services on several occasions. But Thomas Boston loved his people and visited them to plead with them secretly about spiritual things. Very soon the people of Ettrick and those for miles around were flooding into the church on Sundays, and into the minister's house for counsel during the week. Once again we have the practical goodness of a love that was willing to cross the barriers of opposition.

Thomas Boston's preaching always had an evangelistic edge. When he was finally overtaken by illness he insisted on preaching on the Sunday, saying that he had never known a silent Sabbath, and it was too late to start.

So a dying man's deathbed was turned into a pulpit, and the congregation gathered below his window from all the nearby hills and valleys. Even when he was propped up in bed, his goodness was again crossing the barriers of opposition, pleading with men to get right with God.

Every bit of energy went into the phrase, 'Behold the lamb of God.' There was no strength left; only a frail body breathing heavily. The vast crowd drifted silently away to whisper that Thomas Boston was dead, and to acknowledge that a good man had died.

The way goodness works
The third minute particular of the practical goodness of Barnabas is that he walked by faith and not by sight. Some time after being introduced to the disciples at Jerusalem, Paul (still called Saul at this stage) went away into Arabia to spend nine years preparing himself for God's work. At the end of those nine years we find Barnabas in Antioch where the Spirit was moving in a powerful way, and we are told that 'a large company was added to the Lord.' The next few words are important: 'So Barnabas went to Tarsus to look for Saul.' Paul was absolutely untried as a Christian worker. Barnabas had an expanding church on his hands, and something of the practical nature of this man's

goodness is seen in the fact that he realized he was not the right man to be at the head of the work, so he went to look for God's chosen leader. Goodness always walks by faith and not by sight. It is not interested in self appointment, but in God's appointment. No wonder Luke could say that 'Barnabas was a good man, full of the Holy Spirit and of faith.'

Why can't we be good?

Dr Paul Rees was once browsing in a public library looking through a shelf of books on psychology, when the title of one book caught his attention so that he took it down. The book was called, *Why we can't be good?* Dr Rees opened the book to discover a quotation on the flyleaf that read, 'Sin writes history; Goodness is silent.' The author of the quotation was, of course, right; there is nothing more silent than goodness, if we mean goodness in a worldly sense. But if we mean the practical generous goodness of the New Testament, then the author was wrong, for the goodness that the Spirit brings to a man's life writes history and can even make sin silent.

Beware!

There are dangers in living the kind of goodness that makes history – it will provoke opposition and resentment. This is nowhere better demonstrated than by two preachers at Greyfriars in Edinburgh in the last century. The preaching theme for the day was goodness. The preacher in the morning said that goodness is so beautiful that, when Jesus

69

showed the world true goodness, all were immediately attracted to him. The preacher in the evening said that true goodness was seen in Christ, and he went on to say that when the world saw him it wanted to crucify him.

True goodness, as the second preacher rightly showed, brings immediate reaction.

The fruit of the Spirit is . . . faithfulness
Galatians 5.22

For better or for worse

Jesus did not ask his followers to be clever or successful, but he did require them to be reliable and trustworthy. So it is not surprising that we find faithfulness in the list of the fruit of the Spirit.

To fasten oneself to

Strictly speaking the word in Galatians 5.22 is 'faith,' which is one of the most common words in the New Testament, but modern versions of the Bible are right to translate it as 'faithfulness', because the Greek word does include the idea of fidelity. There is also some evidence that the English word 'faith' was originally linked to the thought of personal dependability, for our word probably comes from the Anglo-Saxon *feyth* which has the root meaning 'to fasten oneself to.' We are to fasten ourselves to Christ; this begins with a simple step of faith and continues with a life-long attitude of faithfulness towards him.

One of the best illustrations of this word comes from the Old Testament and shows the faithfulness of Ittai to his king. This happened at the time of the Great Rebellion, when David's son Absalom led a coup d'état to force his father from the throne. Absalom had become so popular with the ordinary people that all David could do was to hurry into exile.

From Jerusalem there weren't many escape routes open to David; the safest was in a north-easterly direction that would take him to the country of Gilead. However, it wasn't the easiest journey to make, for it would include climbing down into the Rift Valley and cutting through the undergrowth that surrounded the Jordan before actually wading across the river. And all this had to be done at speed if the king was to escape the hands of the revolutionaries.

It is difficult to estimate accurately the size of the royal party escaping to exile. It obviously included the loyal members of David's family and personal bodyguard. It probably numbered about a thousand, of which the greater proportion were the foreign soldiers of David's personal security force. David gave these men permission to leave him if they wanted to; but Ittai came to David with one of the most remarkable professions of faithfulness to be found anywhere in the world. He said, 'As the Lord lives, and as my lord the king lives, wherever my lord the king shall be, whether for death or for life, there also will your servant be' (2 Samuel 15.21).

If we look at these words carefully, behind a soldier swearing allegiance to his king we can see exactly what it means to be faithful to Jesus.

The unthroned king

Firstly, it means recognizing the king without a crown. David had to leave his royal palace. He was no longer seated on a throne; and presumably he wasn't wearing a crown or the luxurious clothing of the court. If he knew anything of the hazards of the journey before him, he would be wearing tough, ordinary, outdoor clothing. Yet Ittai recognized him to be the king; without any hesitation he said, 'As my lord the king lives.'

A similar kind of faithfulness is required from us; we also have to recognize a king without a crown. For Jesus laid aside the royal clothes of heaven when he came into this world and put on the rough clothing of the human race. He became a dusty, suntanned Palestinian; and it is his humanity that we see first in the gospel stories.

One of the thieves who was crucified with Jesus actually became a follower while nailed to a cross, simply because of the things that Jesus said and the way he behaved during crucifixion. Yet all the thief actually saw was a fellow Israelite slowly dying from a very painful form of capital punishment.

John Calvin describes the thief's experience: 'How clear was the vision of the eyes which could thus in death see life, in ruin majesty, in shame glory, in defeat victory, in slavery royalty.'

First of all, faithfulness requires the ability to see Jesus like that.

Ready for either

On some old Roman coins there is a picture of an ox standing between a plough and an altar, and underneath is the inscription, 'Ready for either.' That also describes the faithfulness of Ittai, he was ready for whatever his master chose for him. He said, 'Wherever my lord the king shall be . . . there also will your servant be.'

Secondly, faithfulness is serving a king without a country. That is a good picture of our present situation. The world in which we live is part of God's kingdom, but a coup d'état has temporarily put it into the evil hands of the Prince of this world. Of course Jesus isn't in exile in the same way that David was; he still retains sovereignty, authority and power in spite of the invasion of evil. But the invasion means that followers of Jesus cannot rely on blessings all the time, there will be difficult times as well, and we must be ready for either.

In Kampala there is a cross by a roadside that marks the place where the 'martyrs of Kampala' walked to their death in the last century. The martyrs were young page boys who worked for a corrupt and perverted East African king called Mwanga. He wanted the boys for his selfish homosexual pleasures, but they had become Christians and refused his advances.

'You will be burned alive if you refuse', they were told.

In spite of the threats they firmly resisted Mwanga, so eventually 39 boys were chained together and marched off to Namugongo to die. As they marched they were able to sing hymns with obvious joy. They were even merry, for when one tripped over his ankle chain, causing several to stumble and fall, they all laughed.

One after another the boys went to their death wrapped in a mat of reeds. As each one stepped forward towards the fire he was encouraged by the others.

'Only a few moments and then you will be with the Lord. We are allowed to do this because we follow him who carried a cross for us.'

The faithfulness of the boys enabled them to serve a king who was temporarily without his lands. It didn't matter to them if one moment they were singing hymns and the next they had to face death – they were ready for either.

Farewell, sun, moon and stars
Thirdly, faithfulness means following the king without conditions. Ittai said, 'Wherever my lord the king shall be, whether for death or for life, there also will your servant be.' If we are faithful to Jesus, there is no area of life that we can hold back from him. Few followers have been more trustworthy in this respect than Hugh Maskail, who was one of the men of the Covenant in Scotland in 1666. Because of his devotion to Christ he had to flee to the Pentland hills, and after his capture he was put on trial and publicly tortured before being condemned to death as a rebel. When he was taken to the scaffold at Mercat Cross in Edinburgh his last words rang with fidelity to Christ.

'Now I leave off to speak any more to creatures, and turn my speech to thee, O Lord. Now I begin my intercourse with God, which shall never be broken off. Farewell, father and mother, friends and relations. Farewell, the world and all its delights. Farewell, sun, moon and stars. Welcome God and Father.'

We today are much more likely to have to live for our faith than to die for it, and this can be just as difficult! Faithfulness through the everyday temptations and difficulties is just as much a fruit of the Spirit and just as pleasing to God. One of the things we may have to face is hardship.

I lodged in a bundle of straw
Certainly the early church knew nothing of the luxuries that most Christians in the western world take for granted today. If the pioneer missionaries of previous generations had not been willing to suffer hardship, then today we would be living in a totally pagan world devoid of even the civilizing effects of nominal Christianity.

David Brainerd was the first man to take the Christian message to the Indians of North America, and he wrote of his hardships like this:

'I have no fellow Christian to whom I might unburden myself, or lay open my spiritual sorrows. I live poorly with regard to the comforts of this life; most of my diet consists of boiled corn and pastry. I lodge in a bundle of straw, my labour is hard and extremely difficult, and I have no appearance of success to comfort me.'

In our own time there could easily be a call to a new type of pioneer missionary; not one who is asked to go to the other side of the world, but one who is willing to give up a few physical comforts to take the Christian message in a simple way to a society that is discovering that food does not mean satisfaction, education does not mean wisdom, money riches, nor leisure happiness.

Gambling away our lives

Paul refers to his fellow worker Epaphroditus as a man who was willing to risk his life for the work of Christ. The word 'risk' has a remarkable history. In Roman times it was used to describe the most popular type of gambling. One scholar translates it by saying that Epaphroditus *gambled* away his life, but even that is far too polite a way of translating the word that Paul used. To get the full abrasive challenge of this man's life you would have to paraphrase 'risk' as 'bingo.' Such was the faithfulness of Epaphroditus that he was willing to *bingo* away his life for the work of Christ (Philippians 2.30).

The same word is used in the early church to describe a group of Christians who disregarded their own safety to visit the sick, particularly those with infectious diseases. They were at work in the third century when the plague swept through Carthage, causing the inhabitants to flee without caring for the sick or burying the dead. Cyprian urged his congregation to risk their lives by staying in the city to comfort the dying and bury the bodies that carried the infection.

Jesus requires his followers to serve him irrespective of the dangers involved.

Not under but over
Catherine Booth, the wife of the founder of the Salvation Army, was a person who through faithfulness to Christ became victorious in many areas of life. She was a delicate child bedridden at 14 with spinal trouble and again at 17 with infected lungs, yet she became the mother of eight children and had seemingly limitless energy to help her husband during the first 25 years of the Salvation Army. Temperamentally she was timid, and intellectually untaught, yet she went on to be one of the great preachers of the 19th century, occupying many of the famous pulpits of the day.

At the age of 60 a lump in her breast was diagnosed as cancer. Although her health declined over the next two years, her spirit seemed to soar. Just before her death she sent a message to all the members of the Salvation Army throughout the world. She said, 'The Waters are rising, but so am I. I am not going under, but over.'

It is faithfulness to Christ that enables us to ride over the storms of life rather than to be taken through them.

The fruit of the Spirit is . . . *meekness*
Galatians 5.23

With lowly dignity

We are taught with such emphasis at school that adjectives qualify nouns that we forget that the reverse can be true. And the reverse is certainly true when the noun is 'Jesus' and the adjective is 'meek'.

Meekness is not weakness

If we think of meekness without taking Jesus into account, then straight away the picture we get is of a weak, spineless and effeminate quality, but we will never get that idea if we always link meekness with Jesus, for there was nothing in any way weak or effeminate about him. In fact, few men can ever have lived a more strenuous life than Jesus. The variety of his teaching would have intellectually exhausted most men, and he was clearly specially taxed by working miracles. We should also take into account the physical demands of living without a home and of making every journey on foot. However, despite living in this vigorous way, Jesus was clearly unashamed to be called meek, and at all times, not least when he was riding into Jerusalem on an ass, he gave meekness a lowly dignity.

Controlled strength

Perhaps we won't think it so remarkable that Jesus could be strong and meek at the same time if we discover the true meaning of the word. In classical Greek the word closely associated with the one used in the New Testament meant 'the taming of an animal to bring it under control.' Imagine a wild stallion being caught and broken in. By being tamed, the horse loses nothing of its animal magnificence; it is still powerful and strong, but now it is usable. And that is really the main thought behind the word 'meekness.' A meek man loses nothing of his manliness, he simply becomes usable, which is why the Bible can say, 'Now the man Moses was very meek, more than all men that were on the face of the earth.' Moses was a very rugged man with something of the majesty of a tamed stallion about him; he had a controlled usable power, without wildness.

So meekness is controlled strength. A meek man is one who is strong enough to have himself under control in three basic ways, and, as the Bible gives us Moses as an example of meekness, it will be helpful to look at the controlled strength of Moses in these three aspects.

Less than least

Firstly, the meek man is strong enough to have a realistic view of himself. The writer of the letter to the Hebrews says that Moses 'refused to be called the son of Pharaoh's daughter.' In other words, Moses was strong enough to admit his real origin. While everybody else might feel that he was

Pharaoh's grandson, that all the luxury of the state apartments was his by right and that he was destined to become a prince and a ruler in the land, Moses would never have agreed to such a deception. His meekness made him declare that he was no more than the son of an Israelite slave.

Similar strength in us will enable us to admit to the lowliness of our spiritual origin. We will be able to say that we were slaves under the tyranny of sin before being redeemed by Jesus Christ. And if meekness makes us declare our true origin, it will also make us aware of the true nature of all that life has given to us. We won't make the mistake of saying that our position in life is something that we have achieved. Moses didn't say, 'I was a slave, but now I am a prince, look what I made of life.' He simply refused to consider his elevated position and importance.

So meekness not only makes us strong enough to admit what we were, but also strong enough to admit what we are. The meek man is, therefore, the truly humble man: a man whose humility is based, not on hidden pride or neurotic feelings of inferiority, but only on a real assessment of himself. Such a man will be able to say with Paul that he is 'less than the least of all saints.'

When in doubt, take the losing side

Secondly, a meek man is strong enough to have a realistic view of the needs of others. The writer of the letter to the Hebrew Christians said that Moses not only 'refused to be called the son of Pharaoh's daughter,' but also that he 'chose to share ill-treatment with the people of God.'

The meek man is strong enough to put the needs of others before his own comfort. He will share Thomas Ken's rule of life, 'When in doubt take the losing side. Follow the path which leads not to wealth and honour but to loss, privation, contumely.' And that, of course, is exactly what Moses did; he was so concerned by the plight of the Israelite slaves in Egypt that he joined them in order to help them.

We can go back to a greater example than Moses to demonstrate that meekness has this meaning of being willing to identify totally with the needs of other people. For this is exactly what Jesus did; he took the losing side to lift man to the winning side. It is only the truly meek man who can be totally identified with the problems of others.

The one thing that will enable us to be strong enough to be meek is the challenge of Jesus. Tychon of Zadonsk, the Bishop of Novgorod in the 18th century, continually held the life style of Jesus before the Russian ministers and theological students that he taught.

'The Son of God humbled himself for you – can you be proud? The Son of God took the form of a servant, can you seek to rule? He became poor – can you run after riches? He had nowhere to lay his head – can you require magnificent buildings? He accepted dishonour – can you strive after honours? He washed his disciples' feet – are you ashamed of serving your brethren?'

Is the Lord with us or not?

Thirdly, the meek man is strong enough to have a realistic view of God. The writer to the Hebrews tells us that Moses 'endured as seeing him who is invisible.' The truly meek man will clearly see God in every situation; whereas the man who has no meekness will query the presence of God as soon as life begins to get difficult. Just like the Israelites in the wilderness, he will say, 'Is the Lord with us or not?' The meek man will never ask that question because he is strong enough to see God there all the time.

An open mind to be taught

Because of this continual awareness of God, the meek man's mind will always be open to teaching. As David said, 'the meek he will teach his way.' And the actual pattern of living that God will teach the meek man to follow will be vastly different from the pattern of life that the world knows. Dr Shirwood Wirt, in his book *Jesus Power*, says that man has two different options open to him in life. He can either live *Plan A*, in which he hustles to get to the top of everything and ends up at the bottom. Or he can live *Plan B*, which is the Jesus way. Following the option of the Jesus way, a man will start with a realistic view of himself and of the needs of others, and an awareness of the presence of God; therefore there will be no hustling. He will willingly take the lowest place, but he will end up at the top. That is why the beatitudes say, 'The meek shall inherit the earth.'

Fertile soil

It can sound easy to take the lower way; to some it will even suggest that it means giving up the struggle, whereas the real struggle will be to become meek and humble. For to be truly humble is to go against the tide of world opinion and activity. But if we discover the secret of true humility, it will mean the beginning of godliness and an increasing of our faith. Humility comes from the Latin word *humus*, meaning 'fertile soil'; the sort of soil which Anthony Bloom says, 'we no longer notice because we are so used to it, dumb and dark, capable of making good use of the rubbish we tip on to it, capable of transforming our refuse into wealth, of accepting every seed, giving it body, life and growth.'

That is a good description of the meek man. He may not be noticeable but he transforms everything; he gives body, life and growth to all that he does. The meek man, with lowly dignity, shows the real way to live.

Strong hold

The idea for this book began some time ago when I used to work for the Scripture Union in East Anglia. Several times each week I would have to drive home late at night along a dark stretch of Suffolk road. At a particular point on the road the headlights of my car would light up a hotel sign that declared *Temperance Hotel*. It occurred to me then that it wasn't only the word 'temperance' but all the other aspects of the fruit of the Spirit that were equally misunderstood and misused today. The idea for a book began to form in my mind. So as we come to the last chapter of the book, we also come to the place where that book began for me.

The word 'temperance' comes from the word 'strength.' That is why modern translators correctly translate it as 'self-control.' It is interesting to note that on each occasion that it occurs in the New Testament it appears in connection with an experience or revelation of God. When Luke is writing about Paul's meeting with Felix, he says that Paul 'argued about justice and self-control and future judgment' (Acts 24.25). The implication is that man is to take a strong hold on the way that he is living because of God's moral demands on his life now and his judicial demands on him in the future. Peter says that God's 'divine power has granted to us all things that pertain to life and godliness . . . He has granted to us precious and very great promises.' And he goes on to say that we must therefore make every effort to supplement this knowledge with self-control (2 Peter 1.3,4,6). And in the section on the fruit of the Spirit, Paul speaks of a man taking a strong hold on himself as a natural consequence of the Spirit living in him.

When life goes separate from the man

Before we begin to look at self-control in detail, we need to consider the warning that Christopher Fry puts so eloquently into the mouth of Henry II in his play *Curtmantle*. Henry says, 'The day that any man should dread is when life goes separate from the man.' The Christian life must never become divorced from reality. True spirituality is always extremely natural – so natural, in fact, that it can only really be described by using the word 'supernatural'. Therefore, anything that is artificial, warped, or forced is not New Testament Christianity at all.

Paul described the spiritual life by saying, 'We have this treasure in earthen vessels' (2 Corinthians 4.7). This statement shows the two main areas from which our temptations will come. We are going to be tempted to be *materialistic*, wanting to be all vessel and no treasure. Or we will just as easily be tempted to be *mystical*, trying to be all treasure and no vessel. To be mystical is just as wrong as to be materialistic, because it makes us lose touch with reality and therefore makes life go separate from the man.

In work as well as amusement

Because Christianity is this balance of the life of God in the soul of man, self-control is concerned with every aspect of living. That is why B. F. Westcott said, 'There is lack of self-control in work as well as in amusement; in energy as well as in slackness; in high speculation as in vacancy of thought.' This is really what Paul is saying to Timothy in the second chapter of his second letter. In the first seven verses of this chapter Paul presents us with a cameo of the perfectly self-controlled man. So let us look at these verses in detail.

I give thee all

Firstly, in our personal lives we are to have the self-control of a soldier. Our total aim in life must be to obey and satisfy our Commanding Officer (verse 4). John Calvin's crest was a burning heart, with the motto 'I give thee all and keep back nothing for myself.' And that really is a summary of the demands that New Testament discipleship makes on every believer.

Such a life cannot be lived without difficulties. Indeed, Paul says, 'Take your share of suffering as a good soldier of Christ Jesus' (verse 3). The wonderful thing is that the rigour of submitting ourselves to the will of Jesus is, in itself, a fruitful blessing.

In one of Amy Carmichael's books she tells of a child turning over the pages of an old gardening magazine. An article entitled *The Fruitless Apple Tree* caught her attention, simply because that was a problem in her parents' garden. The author of the article said that the solution was to drive a few nails into the trunk of the tree. The little girl showed the magazine to her father, who thought that no experiment could worsen the condition of the tree, so he hammered a few nails home. The following year the tree bore fruit in a most prolific way.

Reginald Wallis, in telling this story at Keswick said, 'Lord, is that the secret of my barrenness? Is that why I so often fail in the day of testing? Is that why temptation has so easily conquered me? Is that why I become a victim of those things that I know do not belong to the new life in Christ? Is that why I have so often failed in bearing fruit to your glory? Is it because I have raised a protest against the nails being driven into this flesh of mine, this wretched ego, this cursed self?'

Self-control is giving up our own desires and trying to discover what our Commanding Officer expects from us in every area of our lives. In our church life as well as our secular life, we are to make certain that we are not falling back into self life or what Paul calls 'entangling, civilian pursuits' (verse 4). We are engaged in a spiritual warfare; there is no escape for the young and no retirement for the old. Self-control in our personal lives, therefore, is the ability to take such a strong hold on ourselves that we will never do anything that will harm the cause of Christ.

More ships destroyed by worm than cannon
Secondly, in our devotional lives we are to have the self-control of an athlete. Paul reminds Timothy that 'an athlete is not crowned unless he competes according to the rules,' and those rules include adequate training (verse 5). If the first mark of Christian discipleship is obedience to Jesus, the second is a personal discipline that corresponds to the life of an athlete. For the athlete, there can be no cheating in competing, and there can be no competing without a programme of training that has brought him to a peak of physical condition. An athlete who goes on to the track, expecting to be sustained by wishful thinking about medals, instead of relying on the ability that training has brought him, is likely to make an absurd spectacle of himself. Yet many Christians venture into life with pious spiritual day-dreams as a substitute for the real spiritual development brought by daily devotions and the rigours of obedience.

John Fletcher, one of the spiritual giants of the 18th century, wrote, 'More ships are destroyed by worm than by shots from the enemy.' That statement is surprising, because the Royal Navy, created by Samuel Pepys, was by this time well on the way to reaching the zenith of its power. Each vessel was such a formidable fighting machine that it seemed absurd that the real foe was not a broadside of enemy cannon, but a worm, and a worm whose destructive powers appeared to be so insignificant and yet was obviously so devastating.

When John Fletcher made this statement he wasn't, in fact, thinking about the Navy, but rather the vulnerability of the spiritual life. The Christian's real enemy so often isn't the Evil One firing a broadside of fiery darts, or raising a boarding party of attractive temptations; rather it is the Evil One gnawing away at the basic fabric of our spiritual lives. A few tiny but well-placed holes in the devotional life of a Christian, and he is spiritually sunk without a shot being fired.

Like an athlete, we are to take a strong hold on the time we take for exercise, because only when we are spiritually fit will we be able to compete according to the rules. Allowing any hole to be made in the time that we take for those exercises that bring true spiritual life and growth, will bring disaster. Self-control in our devotional life ensures that we're always fit to compete.

The soil, the seed, the showers
Thirdly, in our church life we are to have the self-control of a farmer. As Paul tells Timothy, 'It is the hard-working farmer who ought to have the first share of the crops' (verse 6). In an age when most things happen instantly, simply by pushing a button or moving a switch, we need to look at a farmer to give us the balanced view of church life. The temptation is always to be drawn to one of two extremes. On the one hand we are tempted to say that the church's task is so vast

that it can never be done: and, on the other hand, to want to get all the ploughing, the planting and the reaping done in a single day. The balanced view is to accept the divinely appointed pattern of the seasons, and to be the hard-working farmer who ploughs, sows, reaps and then patiently begins the whole process over again.

Like the farmer, we accept the sovereignty of God. We don't imagine we can ever be the creators of spiritual life, neither do we make our lack of creativity an excuse for laziness by leaving the gospel fields unploughed or the seed of the word unsown. If God is sovereign, the church is a steward and hard work is still necessary to soften the soil and sow the seed. Nowhere is God's sovereignty and man's responsibility so clearly seen to be a joint venture than in the church's work. Just as self-control is necessary in our personal lives, and in our devotional lives, so it is also necessary in church life to keep us bent on the task of evangelism.

The church that is not passing on what it has heard (verse 3) is not only going to reap a poor crop, but is also lacking in New Testament self-control.

Softening the soil. The soil is the world, and it still needs cultivation. Where it is hard it can be softened, and where it is intractable it can be broken down. The one thing that is certain is that the church must go to the world rather than expecting the world to come to the church. Whoever heard of a farmer inviting a field to come to his tractor? And yet we continue to be an inviting,

95

rather than an invading, church. If the soil is to be softened we must start invading the world, and for us the invasion begins in our home and with our neighbours, and in our place of employment.

Sowing the seed. Sometimes the furrows that Christian people make are beautifully straight; every large clot of earth has been broken down and even the most minute stone has been removed. Life is lived in the most honourable way. Everything that is right is publicly defended, and every detail of law is painstakingly obeyed. Yet, there is no sowing of the seed. A farmer may prepare his ground with modern machinery, using the most advanced techniques, but there will be no harvest unless he sows the seed. And the same is true for the Christian; the seed must be sown. The truth that we hear Sunday by Sunday, or discover daily from the Word of God, must be sown in the world if there is to be a harvest.

Seek the Showers. D. L. Moody, in his book *Prevailing Prayer*, speaks of the Reformation as the days when 'Luther and his companions were men of such mighty pleading with God, that they broke the spell of the ages and laid nations subdued at the foot of the cross.' In a similar vein he speaks of Richard Baxter 'staining his study walls with praying breath' until he was anointed by the Holy Spirit who sent a river of living water through Kidderminster. Without a doubt the spell of the ages needs to be broken again, and it will only be done when Christian men and women take a strong hold on themselves and begin to cry, 'Down with Heaven!'